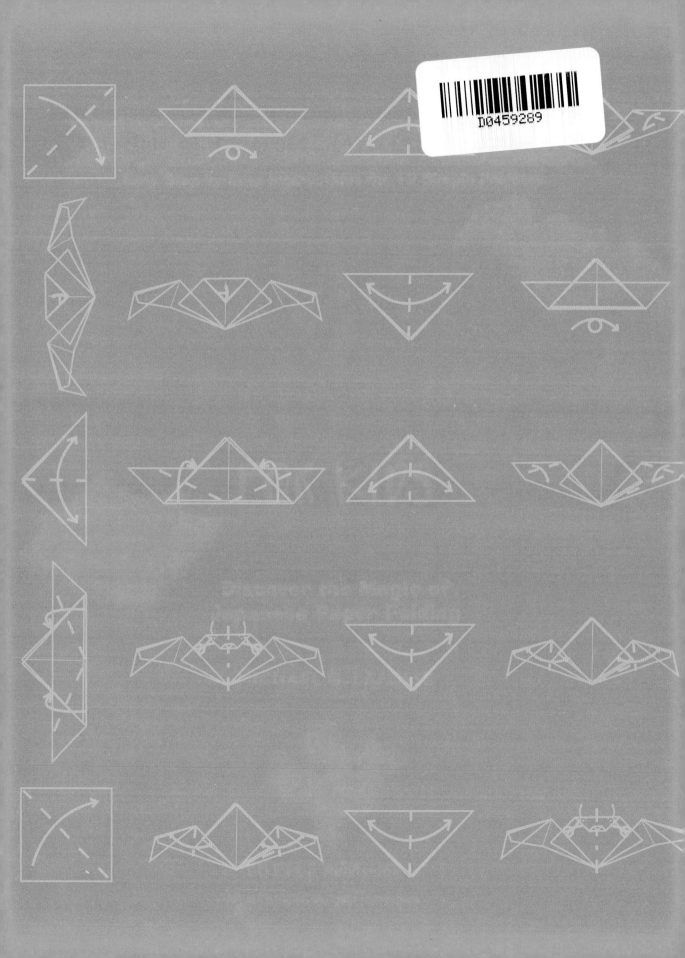

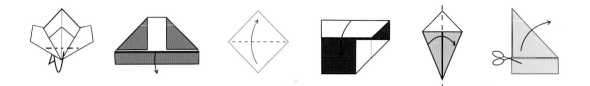

Contents

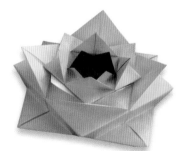

Projects **10**

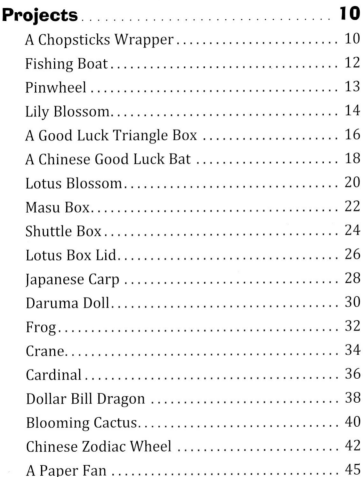

Introduction

The idea of folding materials is an ancient one. Think of the advantages: Folding cloth makes it easy to carry. Folding a letter written on paper keeps its contents secret to the casual passerby. Wrapped in paper, food, medicine, or gifts stay clean and fresh. Documented thoughts, such as stories or journal accounts, are more convenient to carry around and read when the written papers are fanfolded into a book (as opposed to rolling them in long scrolls).

With origami, the paper becomes more than just a wrapper since the design of the folded paper is interesting in some way. Origami is a special type of paper folding that often results in a beautiful pattern, a representation of a living thing, or a familiar or clever object. In Asia, spiritual symbolism has been expressed through folded paper shapes and forms.

One of the wonderful aspects of origami is its simplicity. The folder does not need anything except something to fold—no glue, no tape, no string or wire—just a piece of paper! Though the materials are simple, origami exemplifies the ability of the human mind to solve problems and create beautiful harmony. Folding is relaxing and peaceful, but it is also fun and exciting to invent new ways to fold paper. The satisfaction of producing a work of beauty, or discovering something, such as a form that you have never seen before, can be addictive. Certain folders specialize in creating origami puzzles, or action models—origami that has moving parts, like the Flapping Bird that moves its wings when its tail is pulled—that delights people of all ages.

The Chinese are credited with the invention of paper, and they were probably the first to create folded paper designs. But today, paper folding is known the world over as *origami*, a Japanese word. There are several possible reasons for this, but perhaps the best involves the Japanese origami crane, one of the most popular designs around the world. This folded paper classic is well documented in Japan's history and has been folded for at least 400 years. For many years the paper crane was considered the most advanced model in the world. When modern publishers and promoters of paper folding needed a simple word for the art, they looked to Japan, the home of the folded paper crane, and came up with origami. In Japanese *ori* means to fold and *kami* means paper.

Since papermaking and paper folding began in Asia, the origami projects presented in this book naturally convey aspects of Asian culture. Flip through these pages and you'll discover a world of chopsticks, Koi fish, and good-luck Darumas!

Paper Used for Origami

Since origami is simply the art of paper folding, any paper can be used. However, choosing the best paper for a particular project can be as important as the folding process. Here are some things to consider:

Paper for learning and practicing origami does not have to be fancy or expensive. You should look around for papers that are fairly thin and in good supply, like copier paper or discarded magazines. You can fold any of the projects in this book with these papers. You must, of course, prepare your paper by first cutting it to the proper size and shape for the project (the basic techniques are explained in another section of this book). Cut your papers carefully to make perfect squares, and you will be off to a good start.

Once you have learned the folding method for

Making Paper Squares from Rectangles and Rolls

Most origami projects make use of the square shape as the starting point of design. There are good reasons for this: The square is the easiest shape to make without the use of complicated techniques or special tools, and the shape has a symmetry with many advantages for folded paper design. Other shapes can be used, but they are less frequently encountered. This book uses only square paper designs.

The paper that you are likely to find at hand will not be in the familiar origami square shape. Most paper was made for other purposes such as letter writing, gift wrapping, wall covering, or book, magazine, and newspaper publishing. You can easily prepare such papers for almost any origami project by following these simple steps.

1

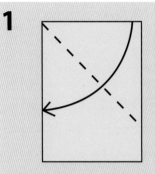

Fold the short edge of a piece of rectangular paper to align with one of its longer edges. Fold carefully—neatness counts!

2

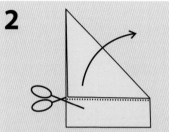

Cut away the paper that extends beyond the edge of the overlapping triangle of paper. You can do this with scissors, or you can simply fold along the edge and then carefully tear the paper away.

3

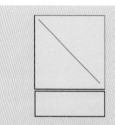

Now you have the largest possible square from this sheet of paper. If you wish to make smaller squares, you can divide the square into quarters, by folding, and then cut along the creases. You can also cut smaller squares from the leftover strip of paper.

4

To make squares from a roll of paper, begin by cutting away a strip as wide as the size square that you will need for your project. Fold and cut a square from this strip in the same way you did with the sheet of rectangular paper.

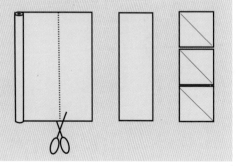

Origami Resource Guide

The Origami Source
c/o Phyliss Meth
40-50 166th Street
Flushing, NY 11358
www.origami-usa.org

Sasuga Japanese Bookstore
7 Upland Road
Cambridge, MA 02140
Phone: (617) 497-5460

www.sasugabooks.com
A great source for Japanese books, origami and otherwise!

Origamido Studio
www.origamido.com
The only origami art gallery studio in the United States. Original origami designs and hand papermaking for origami art.

OrigamiUSA
15 West 77th Street
New York, NY 10024
(212) 769-5635
www.origami-usa.org
origami-info@origami-usa.org
A membership supported, not-for-profit, origami dedicated organization

A Chopsticks Wrapper

Traditional Japanese Design

For thousands of years, long before metal spoons, forks, and knives existed, chopsticks were the simplest, most practical way to handle food. Today chopsticks are still commonly used throughout Asia.

In Asia, special attention to the presentation of food and gifts is common, so items are often wrapped. Visitors often remark that many articles are wrapped at least twice! This paper chopstick wrapper is an easy way to keep chopsticks in sets of two. It allows kitchen staff to set a table without handling the ends of the chopsticks that will touch the diner's food or mouth. Formal dining in Asia often features fine-quality chopsticks presented in clean folded paper wrappers. In Asian markets, bags of colorful folded paper chopstick wrappers hang in plastic bags, often with an origami decoration adorning the package.

What You Need

Use paper that is at least six inches (15 cm) square. White paper is most traditional for this wrapper. Origami paper, colored on one side only, is perfect: The wrapper will be white on the outside with a little bit of the colored side showing from inside the top.

This design displays the red corner presented against the rest of the white paper, and it is considered a variation of the theme used for the Japanese flag. This makes the white surfaces available for calligraphy or special messages. Most chopstick wrappers are folded from rectangles.

Instructions

1

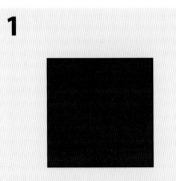

Begin with the colored side up, if you are using origami paper. Fold the bottom edge to the top edge. Unfold.

2

Carefully fold the bottom edge to the crease line and unfold. Repeat with the top edge and unfold.

3

Fold the lower right corner to the center crease. Be careful to align the top edge of the corner with the center crease.

Fold the upper right corner to the first crease from the top. Be careful to align the bottom edge of the corner with this crease.

4

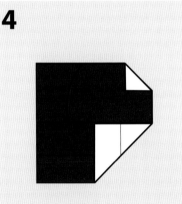

Fold down the top edge to the middle crease.

5

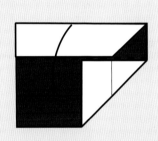

Fold down the top folded edge to the first crease from the bottom.

6

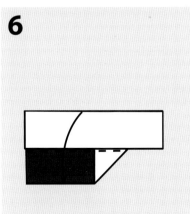

Fold down the top folded edge to the bottom edge.

7

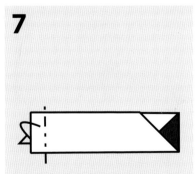

Fold approximately one-half inch (1 cm) of the left end around the back to close the wrapper.

8

The finished Chopsticks Wrapper.

Fishing Boat

Traditional Japanese Design

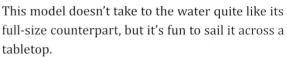

Fishing boats are pleasure craft designed for sport fishing. The raised pilothouse gives the vessel's captain a good view over rough seas.

This model doesn't take to the water quite like its full-size counterpart, but it's fun to sail it across a tabletop.

Instructions

1

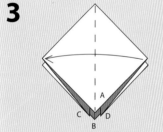

Make mountain folds, corner to corner, and valley folds, edge to edge, on the colored side of the paper.

2

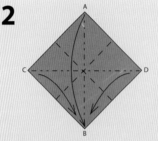

Mountain-fold the C and D corners, bringing C, A and D down to B.

What You Need

A square sheet of paper of any size. If you run out of kit paper, you can use colorful gift wrap. Try racing these across a table with puffs of air.

3

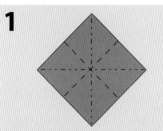

Your paper should look like this. Move the top right corner over to the left.

4

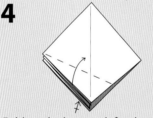

Fold up the bottom left edge and one corner to the front. Look at step 5 for the shape. Repeat behind.

5

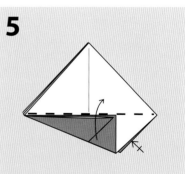

Fold up, front and back.

6

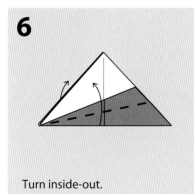

Turn inside-out.

7

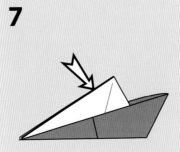

Push in from the top.

8

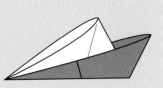

The finished Fishing Boat.

Pinwheel

Traditional Design

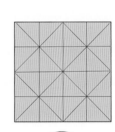

This classic model makes a lovely room decoration, but is most exciting as a dynamic action model, twirling in the breeze. Once folded, loosely attach the center of the pinwheel to a pencil eraser with a thumbtack. Take it for a spin!

Instructions

1

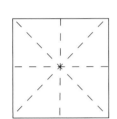

Begin with the white side up. Valley-fold in half, corner to corner and edge to edge, in all four directions.

2

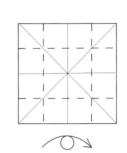

Fold and unfold each edge to the center. Turn over.

What You Need

A square sheet of paper of any size. Try using multicolored papers, and watch how the colors seem to change when the model spins rapidly.

3

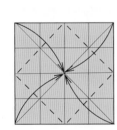

Fold all four corners to the center.

4

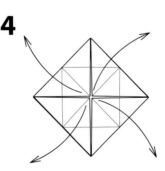

Unfold.

5

Your paper will look like this. Turn over.

6

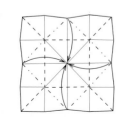

Using the crease pattern, bring the center of all four edges to meet at the middle of the paper. Let each corner fold in half.

7

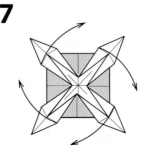

Fold each corner over, clockwise.

8

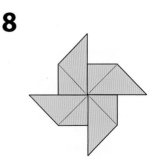

The finished Pinwheel.

Lily Blossom

Traditional Japanese Design

This origami flower is a long-time favorite. Also called an Iris, this design easily presents a stripe on each petal if you leave a slight gap between edges at step 5 when folding two-sided (duo) papers. Make a bouquet by attaching pipe cleaner, florists' wire, or green-paper wrapped bamboo skewer for stems.

What You Need

Use a five- to eight-inch (13 to 20 cm) square of colorful paper for each blossom. Find as many larger green papers to cut or fold simple leaves, and to glue over wires or sticks to make stems.

Instructions

1

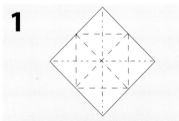

On the white side of the paper, make mountain folds, corner to corner, and valley folds, edge to edge. Valley-fold and unfold the four corners to the center.

2

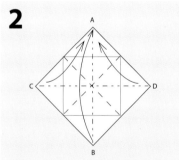

Mountain-fold the C and D corners, bringing B, C and D up to A.

5

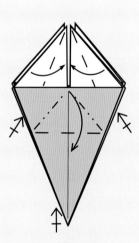

Move the middle edge towards the bottom, while folding in the top edges. Repeat behind, and then with the two inside layers. Look ahead to step 6 for the shape.

3

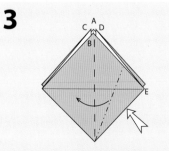

Lift corner E, open the layers and flatten it. Look ahead at step 4.

4

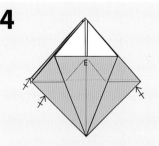

Repeat behind, and then with the two inside corners, turning the layers to reveal them.

6

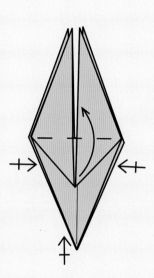

Fold the corner up. Repeat with the other three.

7

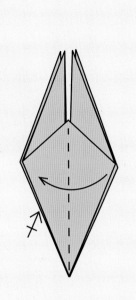

Fold the top layer of the right side over to the left. Repeat behind.

8

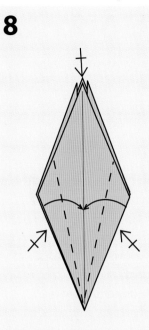

Fold the bottom left and the bottom right edges to the crease. Repeat behind and with the middle layers.

9

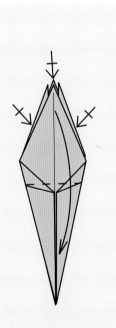

Fold down the front and back petals. Repeat with the other two.

10

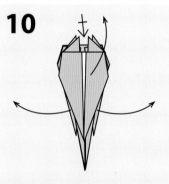

Open petals out.

11

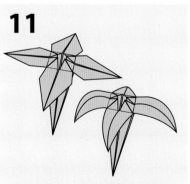

Curl the petals. The finished Lily.

A Good Luck Triangle Box

Design by Richard Alexander,
based on an origami box by Molly Kahn

We give gifts for many reasons. Most often we choose something small, but elegant and handmade if possible, as a true expression of goodwill and friendship. Often a gift is a token of a visit—something that the host or hostess can use to remember the wonderful times spent with good friends and relatives.

Gift giving is an integral part of Asian culture as a way to show thanks and appreciation. In many cultures, superstition influences gift giving and offerings of gifts are made to gods in exchange for a bountiful harvest, or simply for good luck. This box is a great way to present a gift of a small piece of jewelry, candy, a seashell, or another item.

This triangular box is a classic design that is versatile as well as beautiful. Molly Kahn first diagrammed this style of box in America in the early 1950s. This variation was designed in 2002 by Richard Alexander, cofounder of the Origamido Studio in Massachusetts. By pressing the polar corners of the box, it splits open in a way that

What You Need

You will need three pieces of square paper, each the same size, for this project. Six-inch (15 cm) origami paper is ideal. The most festive boxes are made from papers that are colored differently on each side: You could have up to six different colors on one box! Boxes can be made as large or as small as you like, depending upon the size of the paper you begin with.

resembles a fortune cookie. These boxes can easily be strung like beads, hung from a mobile, or even placed as ornaments on a tree.

Instructions

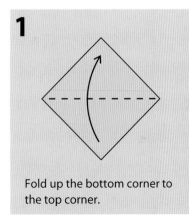

1

Fold up the bottom corner to the top corner.

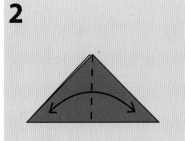

2

Fold in half, right corner to left corner, and unfold.

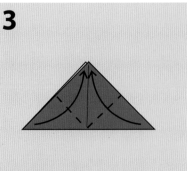

3

Fold up the left and right corners to the top corner.

4

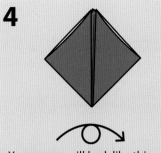

Your paper will look like this. Turn the paper over, from left to right.

5

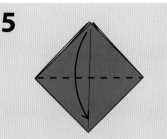

Fold down the top corner of the top layer, carefully matching with the bottom corner.

6

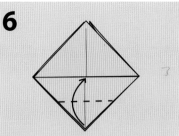

Fold up the bottom corner of the top layer. Make the corner touch the middle of the folded edge at the center of the paper.

7

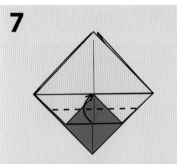

Fold up, folded edge to folded edge.

8

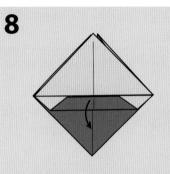

Unfold these folded layers.

9

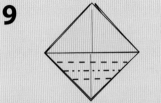

Using the creases as guides, mountain and valley fold up the bottom corner of the top layer to make a decorative band of triangles across the middle of the paper.

10

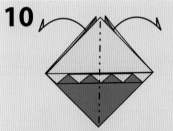

Bring the two corners away from the back. Mountain fold the vertical center crease to make the unit shape ready for assembly.

11

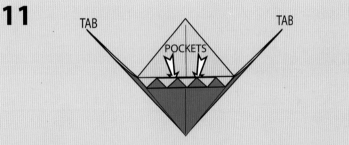

Each unit has two pockets (one on each side of the middle crease) and two tabs (the two outer corners). You will need three units to make one box.

12

Assemble the box by inserting each tab of one unit into one pocket area of another unit. Be sure that all of the valley creases face into the box. If using as a gift box, place a small gift inside after two units are joined. Once all three pieces are arranged, you can push them snugly together to close the box.

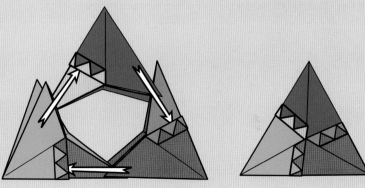

A Chinese Good Luck Bat

Design by Michael LaFosse

T he Chinese language takes advantage of homonyms, words that sound alike but mean different things. The Chinese word for bat (fu) sounds similar to their word for good fortune (fu). For this reason, the image of the bat is commonly seen in Chinese fabrics, drawings, pottery, woodworking, ivory, and other arts. The Chinese consider it good luck if bats roost in your house (maybe because people with bats in their house are less likely to be bothered by insects such as mosquitoes). The Chinese also attach good luck symbolism to the color red, and to the number five, so what could be a better gift than a framed, handmade set of five red bats?

This cute little red bat is fun to make, fun to give, and certainly fun to receive!

What You Need

Use square paper of any size. If you are using heavy, construction-weight paper, you should fold this bat from a triangle shape. Make a proper triangle by folding a square sheet of paper in half, corner to corner, and then unfolding it. Cut the paper in half along the crease line. You will have two triangles to fold bats from.

Create a bat mobile by attaching thread to your bats and hanging them from sticks or wires.

Instructions

1

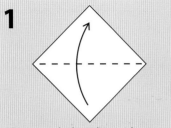

Begin with the white side up, if you are using origami paper. Fold up the bottom corner to the top corner.

2

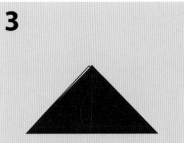

Fold in half, right corner to left corner, and unfold.

3

Fold the bottom edge up approximately two-thirds of the way.

4

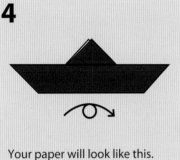

Your paper will look like this. Turn the paper over.

5

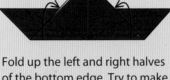

Fold up the left and right halves of the bottom edge. Try to make them touch the intersecting points of the top edges while forming a neat corner at the bottom.

6

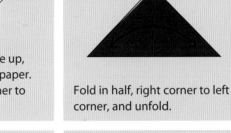

Fold down the top edges of the wing papers.

7

Fold each wing in half. Unfold.

8

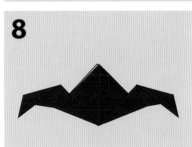

Fold down the top corner, to make the head.

9

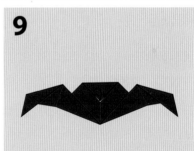

Fold up a little bit of the head corner, to make the mouth.

10

Fold down the nose corner to touch the folded edge of the mouth.

11

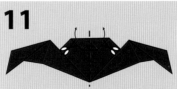

Mountain fold the center crease to make the bat more three-dimensional. (Optional: Cut a diagonal slit in the left and right sides of the head paper. Pull up the free corners to make the ears.)

12

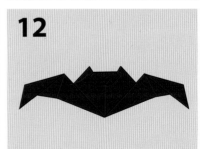

The finished Chinese Good Luck Bat.

Lotus Blossom

Traditional Japanese Design

Throughout many Asian, Indian, and African cultures, the lotus flower has symbolic connections to religious traditions. In Buddhism, the teachings of Buddha are associated with the lotus because it is thought that the universe has layers without end. In Hinduism, it is believed that the lotus flower blossom emerges from the Hindu god Brahma's navel, and at the center blooms another Brahma. In Yoga, practitioners fold their legs in the lotus position for enhanced meditation because they believe when a person breathes, his or her body expands just as a lotus flower blooms. Since the petals of the lotus flower unfold and emerge from the center, it is often compared to a cycle of continuous renewal.

This lotus requires accurate, repeated folding of the corners to the center, called blintzing. This is a great way to develop folding skills—especially precise, crisp, and symmetrical folds.

What You Need

You will need two pieces of square paper, one large and one small, for this project. The large piece should be at least eight and one-half inches (21 cm) and the small pieces should be six inches (15 cm) or less. The two most popular sizes of origami paper, the nine-and-three-quarter-inch (24 cm) and six-inch (15 cm) size, are ideal. Use thin papers.

Instructions

1

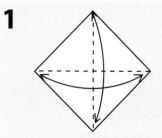

Fold the larger piece of paper in half, corner to corner, both ways to make crossing creases that mark the center of the paper.

2

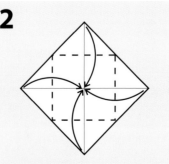

Fold all four corners to the center.

3

Fold all four new corners to the center, covering the four from the previous step.

4

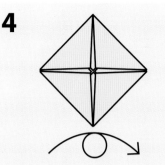

Your paper will look like this. Turn the paper over.

5

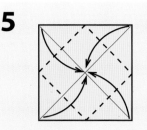

You will notice that the center is still marked by the crossing creases. Fold the four corners to the center.

6

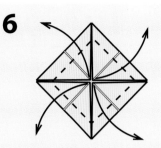

Fold out the four corners so that each goes a bit beyond the edge of the square it is attached to.

7

You now have an eight-pointed star! Turn the paper over.

8

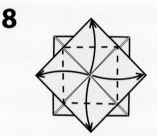

Open the first layer of flower petals by folding the four center corners to their outer corners.

9

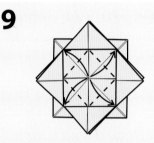

Open the last layer of flower petals by folding the four center corners out flat.

10

Lift all eight petals up a little bit to make the flower look fresh and open.

11

Make a second, smaller lotus blossom, and insert the four bottom corners of the smaller blossom under the folded edges of the center of the larger blossom. They will lock together without the use of glue!

12

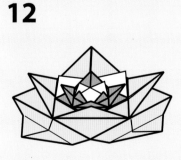

The finished Lotus Blossom

Masu Box

Traditional Japanese Design

T he *masu* is a measuring box. Originally made from wood, it was used traditionally to measure rations of rice and beans. The most ceremonial use of the wooden masu is for drinking sake, a Japanese wine made from rice, especially during their celebration of *Oshogatsu* (New Year's).

This traditional origami box is most often called a masu because it, too, has been used as a measuring box, and it is square like the wooden masu.

We will use the origami masu for the bottom of our three-piece box project. It is perfectly suited for this because it is smooth on the outside, and so the lid will easily slide on. Use any kind of paper, as long as it is the correct size to fit the other pieces of the project. You can use the box alone, however, and if you are folding two, one can serve as a simple lid for the other!

What You Need

Use square paper of any size. Try using colorful papers from magazine covers, gift wrap, old calendars, and scraps of wallpaper.

Instructions

1

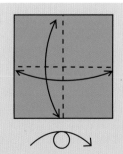

Begin with the colored side up, if you are using origami paper. Fold in half, edge to edge, both ways, to make crossing valley folds on the colored side of the paper. Turn the paper over.

2

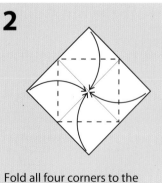

Fold all four corners to the center.

3

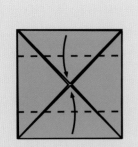

Fold the bottom and top edges to meet at the center.

4

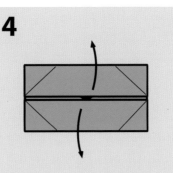

Your paper will look like this. Unfold the previous two folds.

5

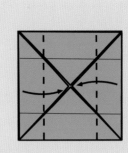

Fold the left and right edges to meet at the center.

6

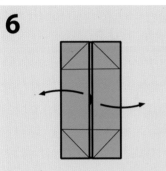

Unfold these two folds.

7

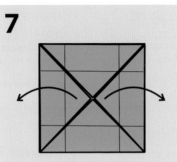

Unfold the left and right corners from the center.

8

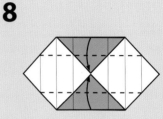

Fold the bottom and top edges to meet in the center of the paper.

9

Turn your paper so that it runs the long way, from top to bottom. Open the folded edges from the center. Look at step 10 for the desired shape.

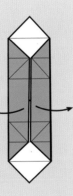

10

Look carefully at the creases in your paper. This folding method has prepared the paper with mountain and valley folds in all of the key places necessary to close up the box shape. Begin by lifting up the left and right walls. Next fold in the four corners a bit.

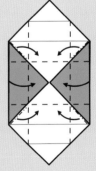

11

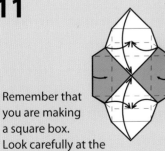

Remember that you are making a square box. Look carefully at the creases and feel how easily they can bend into the right shape.

12

Fold the end flaps up and over the top and bottom walls and into the inside of the box. Lay the corners flat in the bottom of the box.

13

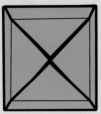

This box needs no glue to keep its shape. Use this box as the bottom to the lotus box project.

Shuttle Box

Traditional Design

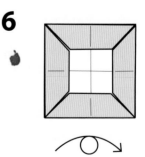

Traditionally, a shuttle is a wooden spool used to weave yarn through a loom. Here it is presented as a sturdy and easy-to-fold box. Use this box to hold small items or to present gifts to friends.

Together the Shuttle Box and the Masu Box make a beautiful and functional gift box, or the Shuttle Box can be used in place of the Masu Box if you prefer this design. Unlike the Masu Box, this box can be made with rectangles other than squares. Try making rectangular versions. The

What You Need

Use any size of square paper. This box makes a good lid for the Masu Box. Use this box together with the Lotus Topper to make a decorative box lid.

Shuttle Box also contains four slots along the sides that are perfectly located to accept the flaps produced by our next project, the Lotus Box Lid.

Instructions

1

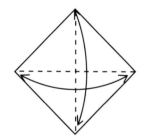

Begin white side up, if you are using origami paper. Fold in half, corner to corner, both ways, to make crossing valley folds.

2

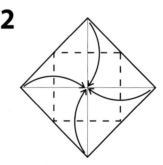

Fold all four corners to the center.

3

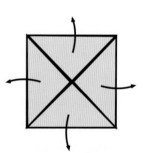

Unfold the four corners.

4

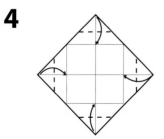

Look carefully at the crease pattern. Fold each corner to the crossing crease nearest it.

5

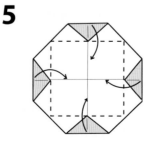

Fold over the four folded edges to make a frame.

6

Your paper will look like this. Turn the paper over.

7

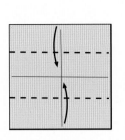

Fold the bottom and top edges to meet at the center.

8

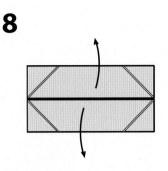

Your paper will look like this. Unfold the previous two folds.

9

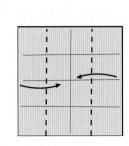

Fold the left and right edges to meet at the center.

10

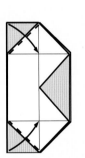

Fold the right top layer to the left like turning the page of a book.

11

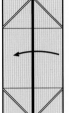

Carefully fold over the top and bottom right corners to the center crease.

12

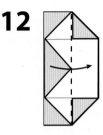

Return the top flap to the right, covering the two folded corners.

13

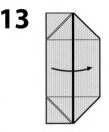

Fold the top left layer to the right side.

14

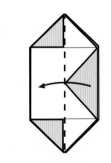

Fold over the top and bottom left corners to the center crease.

15

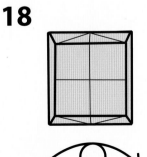

Return the top flap to the left, covering the two folded corners.

16

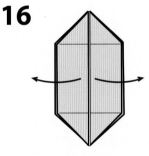

Lift the two center edges up to begin opening the box.

17

Push in the top and bottom corners as you continue to open the box. Sharply mountain fold the outside corners and edges of the box.

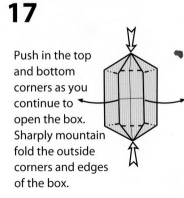

18

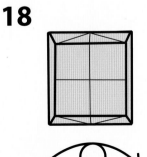

Turn the box over.

19

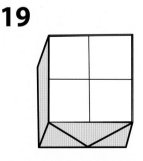

Use this box as the lid for the lotus box project.

Lotus Box Lid

Traditional Design, adapted by Michael LaFosse

In Thailand, there is a celebration called *Loy Krathong*, or the Beautiful Water Festival, celebrated during the full moon, late in the fall. Lotus flower-shaped bowls with candles are floated on the water to draw attention to the importance of pure water.

This lotus decoration and lotus-topped box is a versatile decoration for many celebrations.

This lotus-shaped ornament is made using the same principle as the traditional origami lotus project demonstrated earlier in this book. When folded from paper that is the same size as that used for the Shuttle Box, the four base corners will fit like tabs into the pocketlike edges of the box top. This makes for an easy, glueless construction that is very impressive for a gift box.

What You Need

Use square paper of any size. Thin papers work best. To make the full project—a box with a decorative lid—use three same-size sheets of square paper. From one sheet, fold the Masu Box; from another sheet, fold the Shuttle Box; from the third sheet, fold the Lotus Box Lid. Choose complimentary colors of paper for the three units.

Instructions

1

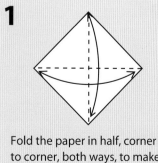

Fold the paper in half, corner to corner, both ways, to make crossing creases that mark the center of the paper.

2

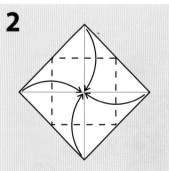

Fold all four corners to the center.

3

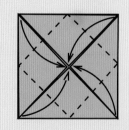

Fold all four new corners to the center, covering the four from the previous step.

4

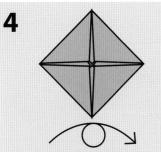

Your paper will look like this. Turn the paper over.

5

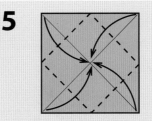

You will notice that the center is still marked by the crossing creases. Fold the four corners to the center.

6

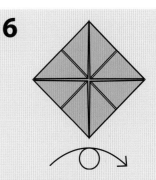

Turn the paper over.

7

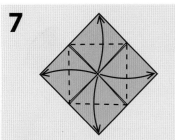

Open the first layer of flower petals by folding the four center corners to their outer corners.

8

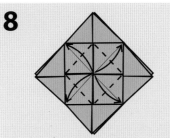

Open the last layer of flower petals by folding the four center corners out flat.

9

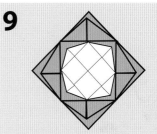

Lift all eight petals up a little bit to make the flower look fresh and open.

10

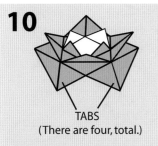

TABS
(There are four, total.)

Four tabs can be found on the underside of this flower. These four tabs fit into the slots on the top edges of the Shuttle Box.

11

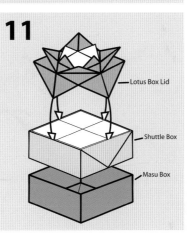

Lotus Box Lid

Shuttle Box

Masu Box

12

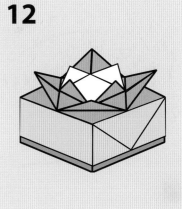

Japanese Carp

Design by Michael LaFosse

The Japanese Carp has red markings on a white body. Since the Japanese national flag is also white with a red circle in the center (symbolizing the rising sun), these fish are popular because they look like swimming flags.

You will note that this project utilizes a scissor cut, not unusual in traditional Asian folded paper figures. We will make use of this traditional technique to create a graceful, forked tail more simply, without the inside-reverse folding we used before. When the final effect is elegant, a cut or two is allowed in traditional, as well as in modern, origami design.

What You Need

Use a square of origami paper, red on one side and white on the other. Any size paper is fine. These Carp are perfect for making a hanging mobile: Attach lightweight thread or fishing line to each Carp, and then hang them from slender sticks of wood or wire.

Instructions

1

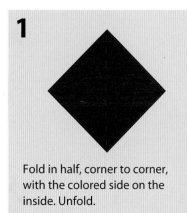

Fold in half, corner to corner, with the colored side on the inside. Unfold.

2

Fold in the bottom left and right edges to meet at the crease.

3

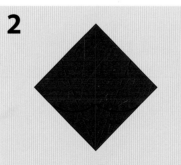

Fold out the two square corners. Look at step 4 for the desired shape.

4

Check the shape. Notice that the bottom edges of the two triangles are in line with each other straight across.

5

Fold in the left and right edges so that the top halves will be parallel to each other and the bottom halves run straight to the corners of the two fins.

6

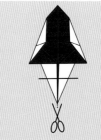

Cut the bottom corner up the middle, a little more than half-way.

7

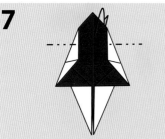

Fold the top corner around the back to make the spot on the head of the Carp.

8

Fold in the top corners to round the outline of the head.

9

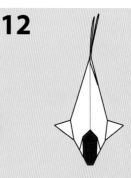

Fold the paper in half and rotate it to look like the figure in step 10.

10

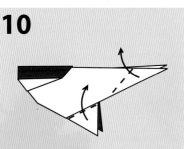

Fold up the two front fins. Fold up one side of the tail.

11

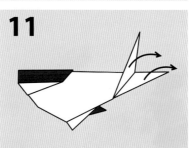

The paper will look like this. (Optional: Curl the tail.)

12

The finished Japanese Carp.

Daruma Doll

Design by Michael LaFosse

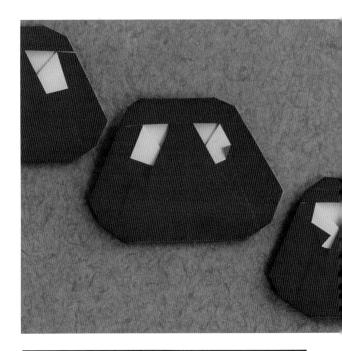

The Daruma is a popular toy in Japan. The toy is based on a famous Indian monk, Bodhidharma, who brought Buddhism to China over fifteen hundred years ago. One story about Bodhidharma tells how he once sat in meditation for almost ten years, his legs wasting away to nothing. So the Daruma doll resembles a red-robed monk with no legs.

The Daruma toys are always sold "eyeless" so that the person receiving the Daruma toy can make a wish by painting in one of the eyes. Legend has it that the Daruma, wanting the other eye, will help the wish to come true. In gratitude for the wish being granted, the recipient of the wish must paint in the other eye.

The Daruma doll is commonly bought at the beginning of the new year, when hope for positive change is highest.

The origami Daruma doll can be used in the same tradition: Make a wish and fold in one eye; when your wish comes true, you can fold in the other eye! This makes for a wonderful New Year activity. Make origami Darumas and mail them to your friends!

What You Need

Use square paper of any size. The traditional colors of the Daruma are red and white so ideally you should use origami paper colored red on one side and white on the other.

Instructions

1

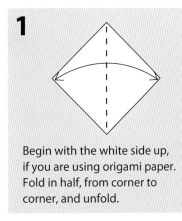

Begin with the white side up, if you are using origami paper. Fold in half, from corner to corner, and unfold.

2

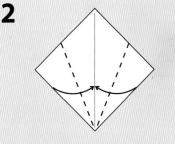

Fold in the two bottom edges to meet at the crease.

3

First fold down the top corner to meet the two square corners, then fold up the bottom corner to touch the middle of the top folded edge.

4

Fold down part of the top layers.

5

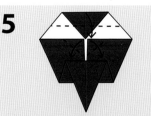

Fold down the top edge to meet at the level of the two square corners. Fold out the two square corners to make paper for the eyes.

6

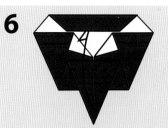

Fold up the bottom corner and tuck it under the top folded edge. This will be the Daruma's nose!

7

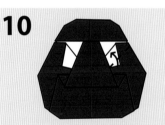

Your paper will look like this. Turn the paper over.

8

Fold in the top left and right edges.

9

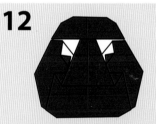

Make the shape more rounded by folding over a little of each of the four corners, as indicated. Turn the paper over.

10

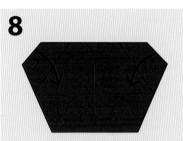

The Daruma is ready to use! First, make a wish and fold over one eye corner to make the pupil show.

11

This is the Daruma doll when a wish has been made.

12

Acknowledge and be thankful to the Daruma by folding over the other eye when your wish comes true!

Frog

Traditional Japanese Design

Frogs are humble, yet charming creatures important in many legends and cultures, often playing the part of the disguised Prince. Origami frogs are artful amusements because they hop when you press the back and release your finger with a backward stroke. Explore paper variations and leg modifications to make it hop higher or farther.

Instructions

1

On the white side of the paper, make mountain folds, corner to corner, and valley folds, edge to edge. Valley-fold and unfold the four corners to the center.

2

Mountain-fold the C and D corners, bringing A, C and D down to B.

What You Need

Use a five- to eight-inch (13 to 20 cm) square. Frogs come in many colors and patterns, so be creative!

3

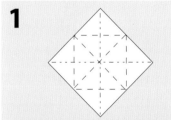

Lift corner E, open the layers and flatten it. Look ahead at step 4.

4

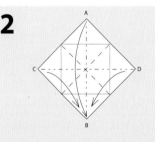

Repeat behind, and then with the two inside corners, turning the layers to reveal them.

5

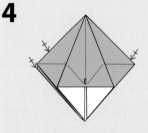

Move the middle edge towards the top, while folding in the top edges. Repeat behind, and then with the two inside layers. Look ahead to step 6 for the shape.

6

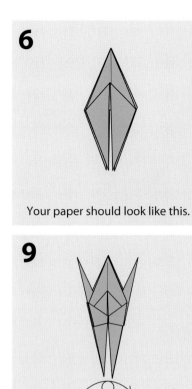

Your paper should look like this.

7

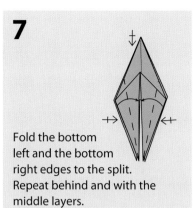

Fold the bottom left and the bottom right edges to the split. Repeat behind and with the middle layers.

8

Inside-reverse-fold, to form the front legs.

9

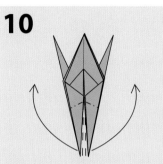

Turn over.

10

Inside-reverse-fold, to form the hind legs.

11

Make inside-reverse folds to form joints in the legs. Look at step 12 for the shape. Blow air into the frog to make it plump.

12

The finished Frog.

Crane

Traditional Japanese Design

The Crane represents the most popular Japanese contribution to origami. It embodies elegant lines, perfect composition, and requires the folder to achieve a certain degree of skill to produce an acceptable model.

The crane has always been an important figure in Chinese, Korean, and Japanese art for many reasons, perhaps the main reason being that they are beautiful birds with long legs, an elegant neck, a slender beak, and large, powerful wings. The crane is a symbol of peace and represents an ideal of quiet strength and beauty, fidelity and faithfulness, and patience. It is considered good luck to see a crane because they often travel great distances and could be gone for a long time.

There is an Asian legend that the crane lives for one thousand years. Since the Japanese developed the folding design for the traditional paper crane, the legend has been extended to

What You Need

Use square paper of any size. Some people challenge themselves by seeing how small an origami crane can they make—the results can be microscopic!

bestow luck and good fortune on anyone who folds one thousand cranes. Certainly, when times were difficult, anyone with the luxury of enough time to fold one thousand cranes was indeed blessed.

Instructions

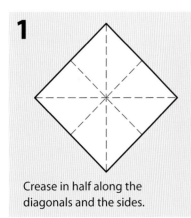

1
Crease in half along the diagonals and the sides.

2
Bring the three corners to meet the bottom corner.

3
In progress...

4

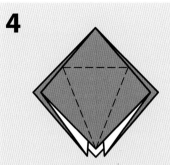

Crease by folding the sides to the center and unfolding.

5

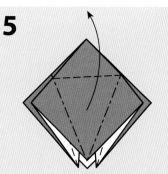

Pull the corner up, allowing the sides to meet at the center.

6

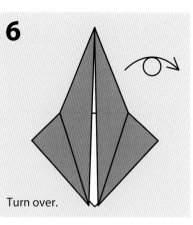

Turn over.

7

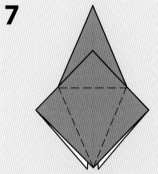

Crease the top section.

8

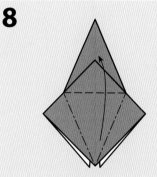

Pull the corner up as in step 5.

9

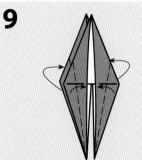

Fold the sides to the center and repeat behind.

10

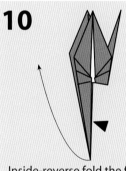

Inside-reverse fold the flap upwards.

11

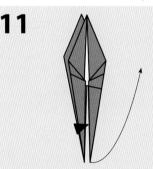

Inside-reverse fold the other flap.

12

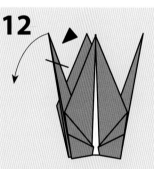

Inside-reverse fold the tip of the flap down.

13

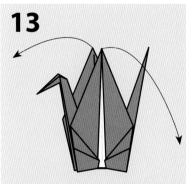

Pull the wings apart.

14

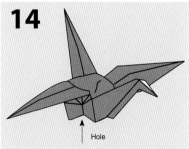

Hole

Completed Crane. You can blow in the bottom hole to give it more volume.

Cardinal

Design by Michael LaFosse

T he North American Cardinal is nature's exclamation point, both in color and in song. These delightful birds often stay behind in the snowy North during winter, bringing cheerful entertainment to so many people with backyard bird feeders.

What You Need

Use a six- to ten-inch (15 to 25 cm) red square with black on the back. If you have white-backed red, you need only color only ¼ of the back (the head area) with black.

Instructions

1

Fold in half, edge to edge each way, to mark your paper with crossing creases.

2

Fold the top edges to the crease lines and unfold. Fold the top corner to the center of the back and unfold. Use these mountain and valley creases to bring A, B and C together.

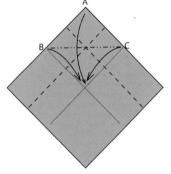

3

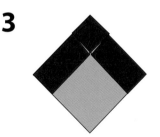

Your paper should look like this. Fold over the right corner at the top square.

4

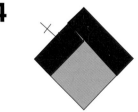

Fold the cut edge to the folded edge while mountain- and valley- folding the upper square area. Repeat on the other side.

5

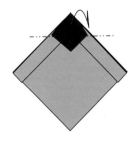

Fold the top corner to the back, letting A move to the top.

6

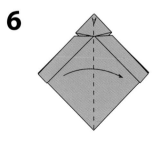

Fold in half.

7

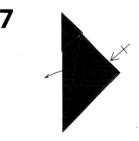

Fold right corner over. Repeat behind.

8

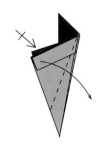

Fold corner down. Repeat behind.

9

Mountain-fold bottom edge inside. Repeat behind.

10

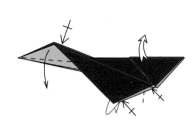

Fold tail papers down on each side. Pull up on the crest of the head, letting the paper in the neck fold up to show the black color. Fold under the bottom corners.

11

Fold up the bottom corner of the head. Unfold and repeat behind.

12

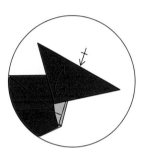

Fold the bottom right edge up to the crease then fold up again. Repeat behind.

13

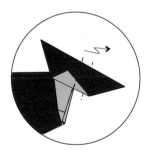

Mountain- and valley- fold the front corner to form the beak.

14

The finished Cardinal.

Dollar Bill Dragon

Design by Michael LaFosse

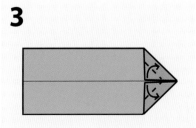

W hether Chinese, Korean, or Japanese, Asian dragons are thought to live in the water and fly through the air. In Asian myths and traditions dragons are capable of bringing rain and creating thunder with their battles in the sky.

Dragons are often associated with themes of renewal, and perhaps for this reason the traditional Chinese New Year celebration always features the Dance of the Dragon. In this dance several people dress up in a dragon costume and dance in a human chain. Together they become a large serpentine dragon with the lead person controlling the fierce head, raising and lowering it to excite the crowd.

Use a dollar bill instead of regular origami paper to create this project. In Asia, paper money is often integrated into art or craft items that are given as gifts or religious offerings to the local Buddhist temple, and they can be disassembled

What You Need

Use a crisp, new dollar bill. Other denominations are fine, too, especially if the dragon is to be a gift of money. You can fold this dragon from any rectangular strip of paper, which is a good way to practice the model before using real money. And longer rectangles make longer dragons! You can try using paper money from other countries, too.

when the money is needed. Paper money specially printed for the purpose is ceremonially burned as an offering to one's ancestors. It is believed that the burned money will be sent to the spirit world and to the deceased.

Instructions

1

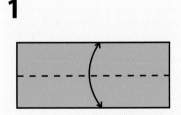

Fold in half, from long edge to long edge. Unfold.

2

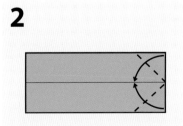

Fold in the top and bottom corners of the right side. Be sure to align their edges with the center crease.

3

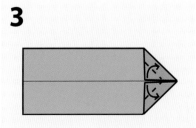

Fold out the two corner points. Make each point touch the middle of its folded edge.

4

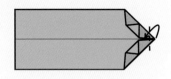

Fold over the right corner to make the nose.

5

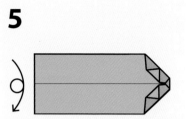

Your paper will look like this. Turn the paper over.

6

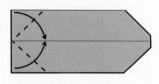

Fold in the top and bottom corners of the left side. Be sure to align their edges with the center crease.

7

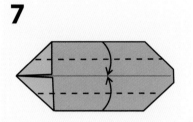

Fold in the top and bottom edges to meet at the center crease.

8

Fold in the top and bottom angled edges of the left end to make the tail thin.

9

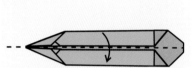

Fold entirely in half, from the top edge to the bottom edge.

10

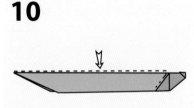

Inside-reverse fold the full length of the body. Look at step 11 for the desired shape.

11

Make the body snakelike using a series of inside-reverse folds. Look at step 15 for a suggested shape, but you may make a different shape if you wish. Follow the close-up details to finish the head.

12

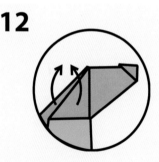

Pull up the triangle flaps to make the horns.

13

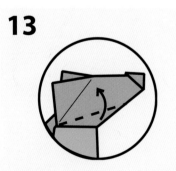

Fold up the bottom edges of the jaw to make the whiskers.

14

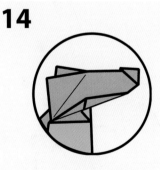

The finished dragon head.

15

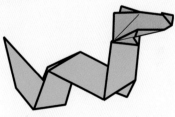

The finished Dollar-Bill Dragon.

Blooming Cactus

Traditional Japanese Design

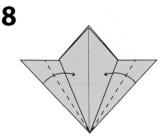

Inspired by cacti with flat, branching pads, this multi-piece origami project will allow you to compose your own flowering cactus branching arrangements. Brighter pinks, reds, oranges, or yellows make stunningly attractive blossoms, just as you would see in the desert after a drought-ending rain.

Instructions

For the blossom:

1

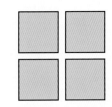

Cut paper into quarters, approximately three inches square. You will need at least six pieces of paper for the cactus plant and three or more pieces for the flowers.

2

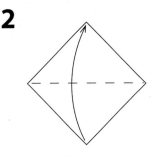

Fold in half, bottom corner to top corner.

What You Need

You will need at least 6 to 8 squares of three- to four-inch (8 to 10 cm) green paper for the cactus plant, and 3 or more squares of the same size for the brightly colored flowers.

3

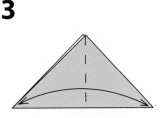

Fold in half, corner to corner. Unfold.

4

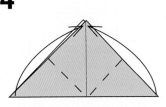

Fold up the left and right corners to the top corner.

5

Turn over, left to right.

6

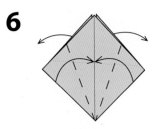

Fold in the bottom left and right edges, allowing the corners at the back to come out to the front.

7

Turn over.

8

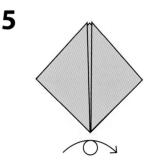

Fold in the left and right edges, covering some of the center shape.

9

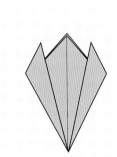

The finished Blooming Cactus blossom.

10

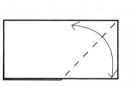

Begin color side up if using origami paper. Fold in half, bottom edge to top edge.

11

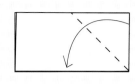

Fold down the right side of the first layer, matching it to the bottom edge.

12

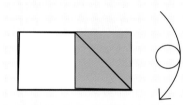

Turn over, top to bottom.

13

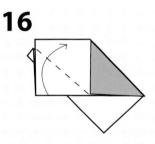

Fold up the right edge, matching the top edge. Unfold.

14

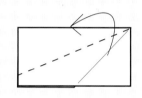

Fold up the right side, matching the crease to the top edge.

15

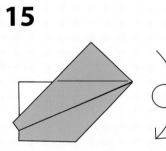

Turn over, top to bottom.

16

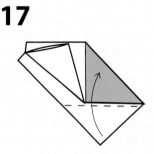

Fold up the left corner. Make sure that the crease runs from the square corner of the triangle flap up to the notch on the left.

17

Fold up the bottom corner.

18

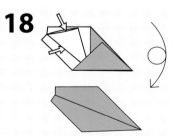

The finished Blooming Cactus base. There are two places where you can fit other pieces into the back. Turn over to see the front side.

19

Be creative! Fit together as many segments as you like, adding cactus blossoms at the ends. You may use glue to make your cactus design permanent.

Chinese Zodiac Wheel

Design by Michael LaFosse and Satoshi Kamiya
Inspired by designs by Paulo Basceta and Mette Pederson

This project uses twelve pieces, a number that represents the animals of the Chinese zodiac. These animals are a rat, an ox, a tiger, a rabbit, a dragon, a snake, a horse, a sheep, a monkey, a rooster, a dog, and a pig. These twelve animals follow a twelve-year cycle. Discover which animal you are by finding the animal that corresponds with your birth year in the chart below.

The twelve pieces of this model also represent the twelve months of the year, which makes it a great project to fold as you celebrate the new year. This project is a wonderful frame for displaying an object in its center or, if made large enough, it can be a crown for your head. When made with alternating colors, it can be an exciting composition, like dragons chasing each other, or elephants walking in circles, each joined by trunk and tail. Decorative Chinese borders and carvings around frames, windows, and doorways often have interwoven elements similar to these folded pieces.

What You Need

You will need twelve pieces of square paper, all the same size. You can make small wheels from smaller papers and large wheels from larger papers. The final size of the wheel will be the same size as the square you start with, so twelve sheets of six-inch (15 cm) paper will make a six-inch wheel. A classic color combination is red and gold, but you can try all kinds of color combinations. Try six each of two colors, four each of three colors, three each of four colors, and even twelve colors! Choose colors that represent the season or a special holiday.

 **Mouse** (1948, 1960, 1972, 1984, 1996, 2008, 2020, 2032)

 Dragon (1952, 1964, 1976, 1988, 2000, 2012, 2024, 2036)

 Monkey (1956, 1968, 1980, 1992, 2004, 2016, 2028, 2040)

 **Ox** (1949, 1961, 1973, 1985, 1997, 2009, 2021, 2033)

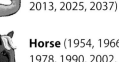 **Snake** (1953, 1965, 1977, 1989, 2001, 2013, 2025, 2037)

 Rooster (1957, 1969, 1981, 1993, 2005, 2017, 2029, 2041)

Tiger (1950, 1962, 1974, 1986, 1998, 2010, 2022, 2034)

 Horse (1954, 1966, 1978, 1990, 2002, 2014, 2026, 2038)

 Dog (1958, 1970, 1982, 1994, 2006, 2018, 2030, 2042)

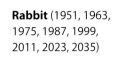 **Rabbit** (1951, 1963, 1975, 1987, 1999, 2011, 2023, 2035)

 Ram (1955, 1967, 1979, 1991, 2003, 2015, 2027, 2039)

 Pig (1959, 1971, 1983, 1995, 2007, 2019, 2031, 2043)

Instructions

1

Begin with the white side up, if you are using origami paper. Mark the middle of the right edge of the paper by folding it in half, from bottom edge to top edge.

2

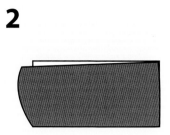

Make a short pinch fold at the right. Unfold.

3

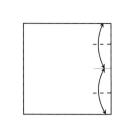

Mark one-quarter divisions with pinch folds by folding the top and bottom edges to the middle pinch mark. Unfold.

4

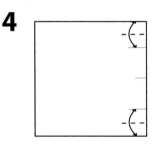

Make one-eighth divisions with pinch folds. Unfold.

5

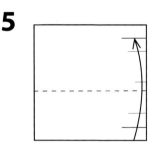

Fold up the bottom edge to the top-most pinch mark.

6

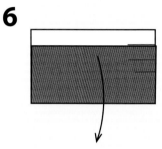

Your paper will look like this. Unfold.

7

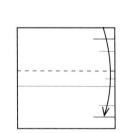

Fold down the top edge to the bottom-most pinch mark.

8

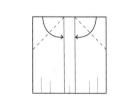

Your paper will look like this. Unfold and rotate the paper so that the pinch marks are at the bottom of the paper.

9

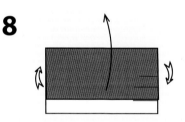

Fold the left and right top corners to the creases, each to the creases nearest to its own side. Be sure to neatly align the edges of the paper to the creases.

10

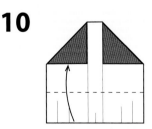

Fold up the bottom edge of the square to the bottom edges of the folded triangles.

11

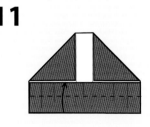

Fold the bottom rectangle shape in half, from the bottom edge to the top edge.

12

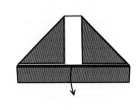

Unfold the bottom layers.

13

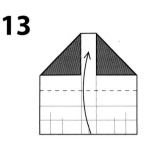

Bring up the bottom edge to the topmost crease. Look at step 14 for the desired shape.

14

Your paper should look like this. Turn the paper over.

15

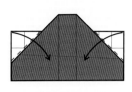

Fold over the two square corners.

16

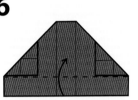

Fold up the bottom edge, making the fold run along the bottom edges of the triangle shapes.

17

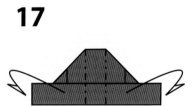

Mountain fold the center parallel creases, bending the left and the right sides so that the folded unit is square.

18

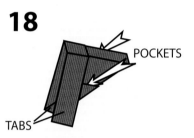

POCKETS

TABS

Note that each unit has two tabs (the square ends) and two pockets, one on each side.

19

When you have made two units, the tabs of one unit will slide into the pockets of the other, one on each side.

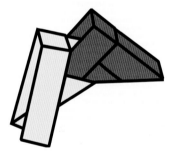

20

Push them together until they are snug. Add each new unit to the pocket end of the growing puzzle. You can use as few as nine or as many as fourteen units to make a ring. Twelve units make a great decoration for any New Year celebration.

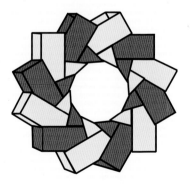

A Paper Fan

Traditional Japanese Design

Regions of Asia are hot and humid, so a fan is an essential item for comfort during the hottest time of the day. People also use fans to build fires and to dry things. Long before paper was invented, the first fans were probably just paddles fashioned from plant leaves, papyrus, or bird feathers by people living in the desert. The first folding paper fans were made in Japan during the eighth century, and they had important ceremonial uses.

A folding fan is easily transportable. Its springlike quality means it nearly opens itself when coaxed, and its lines have a decorative appeal, making a pleasant display on a wall or shelf when not in use.

This project is an elegant, self-locking origami fan, and it is also a great way to practice your essential folding skills. Small examples serve as chopstick rests. Larger ones can be decorated with drawings, paintings, writings, or origami—either before or after folding.

What You Need

Use a square sheet of paper of any size. Small fans, folded from four- to six-inch (10 to 15 cm) paper, make good chopstick rests. Larger fans, folded from ten- to twenty-inch (25 to 50 cm) paper, are nice for displays or for cooling yourself.

Instructions

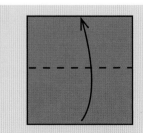

1 Fold in half, bottom edge to top edge, with the display side (colored or decorated side) on the inside.

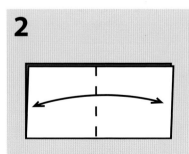

2 Fold in half, short edge to short edge. Unfold.

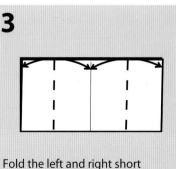

3 Fold the left and right short edges to meet at the crease in the middle of the paper. Unfold.

4

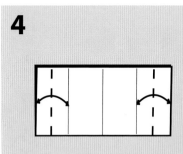

Fold the short edges to the new creases, each to the crease on its own side. Unfold.

5

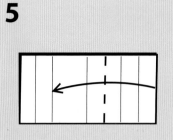

Fold the right edge to the second crease from the left edge.

6

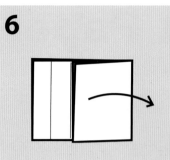

Your paper will look like this. Unfold.

7

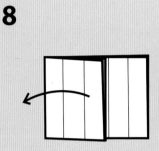

Fold the left edge to the second crease from the right edge.

8

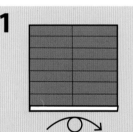

Your paper will look like this. Unfold.

9

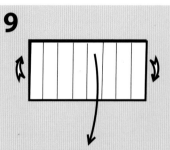

Unfold completely and rotate the paper so that all of the creases except one run horizontally.

10

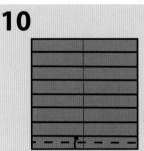

Fold up the bottom edge to the first crease.

11

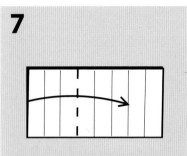

Your paper will look like this. Turn the paper over, from left to right, keeping the folded edge at the bottom.

12

Fold up the bottom folded edge, bending the paper at the crease.

13

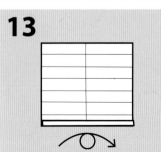

Your paper will look like this. Turn the paper over, from left to right

14

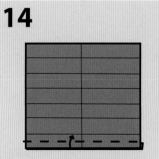

Fold up the bottom edges and align them with the next crease.

15

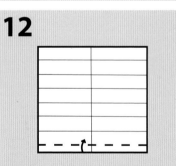

Continue turning and folding the paper to make a series of alternating mountain and valley creases.

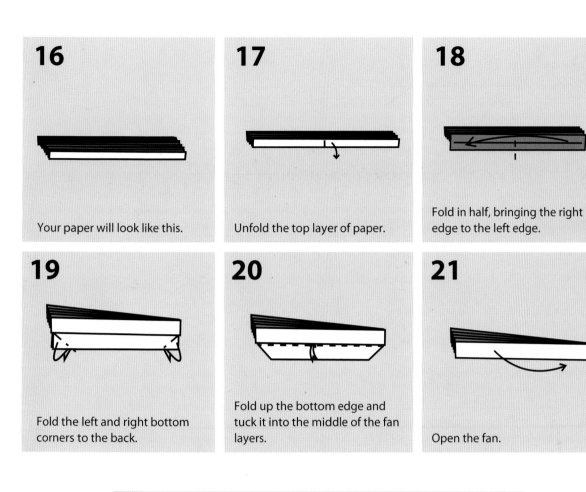

16

Your paper will look like this.

17

Unfold the top layer of paper.

18

Fold in half, bringing the right edge to the left edge.

19

Fold the left and right bottom corners to the back.

20

Fold up the bottom edge and tuck it into the middle of the fan layers.

21

Open the fan.